Ants and Lotus

Ants and Lotus

Poems by

Usha Akella & Ruxandra Cesereanu

© 2026 Usha Akella & Ruxandra Cesereanu. All rights reserved.
This material may not be reproduced in any form, published,
reprinted, recorded, performed, broadcast,
rewritten or redistributed without the explicit permission
of Usha Akella or Ruxandra Cesereanu.
All such actions are strictly prohibited by law.

Cover design by Shay Culligan
Cover image by Petre Nicolescu
Author photo for Usha Akella by Anannya Akella
Author photo for Ruxandra Cesereanu by Corin Braga
Vector image by Amisha Bhatnagar on Unsplash

ISBN: 979-8-90146-803-6

Kelsay Books
502 South 1040 East, A-119
American Fork, Utah 84003
Kelsaybooks.com

We've made many crossings, I hope.
—Usha Akella, "Immigration"
***

*Let's play poetry like a ping-pong
with pencils and books on fire.*
—Ruxandra Cesereanu, "Names II"
***

Acknowledgments

I hope, many bridges spring from the hearth of this book to numerous poetic landings. This poetry above all is tilling in the soil of dialogue.

My gratitude is naturally first extended to Ruxandra, the co-creator of this epistolary experiment. For walking the walk, talking the talk, listening—and—responding. For pouring her creative input with a steely faith in Poetry that is the hallmark of her writing. For not giving up even when fatigue overcame our efforts especially in the publication process. I gained a friend, even as I gained poetry—again.

To Dinu Flămând and the organizers of the Bucharest International festival I am indebted; without the invitation I would never have met a group of Romanian poets in Romania, forged friendships—and unforgettable memories, of which the marked testament is *Ants and Lotus*.

To this list I add Andrei Zanca, a friendship whose seed never sprouted fully. My happiness for the forewords and blurbs by Andrei Codrescu, Magda Cârneci, Basudhara Roy, Zoran Anchevski, Kirun Kapur and Sukrita Paul Kumar comes from deep admiration of the minds and work of these poets.

To Pramila Venkateswaran—my abiding creative companion—my gratitude for proof reading the manuscript. My most sincere appreciation of all those who supported the book in one way or other.

And now, to Kelsay Books and its teams: In a world in which dialogue seems impossible, this is a small ray of hope. My gratitude to KB for making this a reality. Thank you for bringing this book to light.

—Usha Akella

I thank my friend and writer Andrei Codrescu for reading this book in the manuscript stage and advocating enthusiastically for its publication.

I also thank Ioan Cristescu and Dinu Flămând for making possible the poetic meeting between me and Usha at the Bucharest International Poetry Festival in 2019.

I thank Magda Cârneci for being a poetic link between me and Usha when we started this book.

In memoriam, I want to mention here Andrei Zanca, an inspiring poetic and soulful catalyst both for me and Usha at the Bucharest International Poetry Festival in 2019.

And finally, precisely because she is the most important in this poetic project, I thank Usha for her complete dedication to our book and for her indefatigable belief that our manuscript will one day see the light, as it is now.

—Ruxandra Cesereanu

Introduction

In 2019, Usha Akella traveled to Bucharest to attend the international poetry festival, and her encounter with Romanian poetry began; she had met Dinu Flămând at the Trois-Rivières poetry festival the previous year who was instrumental in facilitating her invitation to Romania after he heard her poetry. At the festival, she met Magda Cârneci and Ruxandra Cesereanu. Usha gifted *The Rosary of Latitudes* to Ruxandra. A friendship was initiated.

The impact of regime on creative process and output began to interest Usha as she witnessed the strange sight of communist era buildings embedded in modern architecture on Victoria Street—and listened to Romanian poetry at the festival. Usha's grandfather Nidamarthy Aswini Kumar Dutt and his brother Nidamarthy Uma Rajeshwar Rao had been involved in Communism as a movement, as well as deeply involved in Telugu translations of Russian literature. On the contrary, Ruxandra's paternal grandfather was a political prisoner during the Romanian Communism, with 6 years of prison, because of his religion (he was a Greek-Catholic priest).

The idea of pairing a Romanian woman poet with a South Asian woman poet was seeded soon after; allowing a long-distance communication to burgeon without rules or parameters to see what would happen. Initially, three pairs of poets were formed but eventually only Ruxandra and Usha carried the idea forward.

First, Ruxandra sent Usha a few of her poems translated by Adam J. Sorkin and Paul Doru Mugur.

The epistolary manuscript via email literally flowered from a semantic exploration of names in the first poem. On Friday, June 14th, 2019 Ruxandra wrote her first poem 'As a Lily' and emailed it to Usha while reading *The Rosary of Latitudes*. She followed with a second poem "As a Lily 2" on Sunday, June 16th, 2019. The manuscript was birthed with those two poems. The process of writing in response to each other's work had begun. The first few poems were random and spontaneous between Usha and Ruxandra stemming playfully from the correspondence itself.

In September 2019, Ruxandra lost her mother; devastated by the loss, the mourning seeped into the correspondence, began to fuel the poems, and became the first thematic thread of the collection—the mother metaphor dominated the poems.

The poems meandered through the lens of larger events such as the pandemic and the Ukraine-Russia war. The poems became a lens in turn to inner and outer landscapes—fierce, bereaved, celebratory, and imbued with love for words and life. Life and death are sung in the poems over and over again as real-life losses shadowed the poems—literal loss, personally, globally, and emotionally.

A triumph of friendship and poetry, no such undertaking between two women poets from India and Romania exists in the Literary history of both the countries. The collection of poems halted on March 21, 2022. Only two poems in the manuscript have been prior published ("Joysmos" & "Ants.")

Towards a Religion of Poetry

What you will find in this book is a wonderful meeting between two women poets coming from two different parts of the world: Ruxandra from Romania and Usha from India/United States. Nothing would have destined these two women to get together, yet as a matter of fact I witnessed their meeting in the city of Bucharest during a poetic festival in 2019, which gave birth to an inspirational fusion of two different sensibilities, two different literary discourses, and two different cultures.

What you will read in these pages is a passionate poetic exchange between two strong and gifted women who decided to let themselves open to the influence of the other through the power of words charged with high emotional and visionary forces.

Usha and Ruxandra partake in their poems similar obsessions and traumas related to a woman's destiny—remembrance of childhood, love and birth, loss of the mother, loss of a country or of a clear-cut identity, the invisible presence of our ancestral roots, continuity of life and tradition, opening to the transcendence—which they manage to convey in an astonishing and courageous manner.

Coming from very distant parts of the world, Ruxandra and Usha manifest the same exceptional trust in the magic of poetry, able in their view to fertilize the psyche, to harmonize our being with the nature and the cosmos, to overcome cultural conditionings.

Through the force of daring and ingenious metaphors, they hold together two different spiritual universes, one of Christian origin, the other with deep Hindu roots, that start to vibrate together in the sense of a new spirituality to come.

Playing with words like shamans or goddesses, Usha and Ruxandra hold a tremendous faith in the force of poetry to heal individual wounds and community evils, and to help humanity to transcend towards a cosmic version of itself. That is why they deserve to be read, listened to, and believed as precious heralds of a possible future religion of poetry.

—Magda Cârneci, Romania
Poet, Novelist, Essayist

Elemental Dance
of Spontaneities and Epiphanies

An engaged creative collaboration between two committed artists is like a wild meeting of rivers—unplanned but destined. At the confluence is an ineffable energy, an unfathomable adrenaline rush that animates perception with a clarity which transfigures experience, once and for all.

For rivers that have stuck to their courses, resolutely traversing mountain, plateau, forestland and savannah with equal benignity, the intravenous knowledge of faith and endurance comes through a relentless testing of the world's postulates against their skin. At the confluence, such abrasion transforms into the pure gold of communication as narratives cross fertilize and empower each other, birthing truth and transcendence.

In the impassioned poetic communion between Usha and Ruxandra across these pages, one witnesses a spectacular meeting of two fine souls in loyal and complete abandonment to the principle of poetry, eager to embrace both the pain and the jouissance of the process of unselfing and the reconstruction of the spirit.

There is no reining or hoarding of the self here; only an overarching desire to stretch its limits across differences by bringing lands, histories, imaginations and worldviews in dense conversation with each other. As words travel like ions between these poets in whirls, waves and eddies, their poems become arcades through which our shared vulnerability and potential human strength can be reassessed and reaffirmed.

The reading of these poems, like the writing of them, has to be rigorous self-work, an attempt to widen the frontiers of knowledge, experience and intuition to accommodate the realities of a world that is growing more different, difficult and destitute each day. Nourishment, in such circumstances, can only come from an osmosis between the self and the other.

Stepping into the confluence of *Ants and Lotus* is like participating in an elemental dance of spontaneities and epiphanies. Here luminescence—celestial, aerial, oceanic and terrestrial—unfurls in its full glory. I invite you to be a part.

—Basudhara Roy, India
Poet, Academician, Essayist

Contents

As a Lily (I)	21
As a Lily (II)	22
Names (I)	23
Names (II)	24
Names (III)	25
Joysmos	26
Ushas	28
Lotus	30
The Lost Lotus Found	32
Both	34
Ants	35
The Lotus from Which I Ran Away	37
Rise Lotus, Rise Mother	39
Manthana	40
This Is That	41
A Poem About a Poem	42
Yesterday, my friend,	43
Lullaby	46
Between Us	48
Windows and Doors	50
Piebald	52
Questions	55
Hello from America	56
Hello, Goddess!	57
Map of the Mother	58
9 Days of Poetry	68
Dredge	71
A Lost/Forgotten Poem	73
Then Lights Arose in Memory	74
Lantern	76
Aialik	77

Bodies of Poems	78
Meet Me in the Mirror	79
Whirlpools	80
Meru	81
The Show Must Go On	82
Menhir	83
A Killer Instinct	84
Happy New Year	85
What Else Can Be Said	86
Until I Reach the Last Letters It Is a Way of a Life or Two	87
Adults in Conversation	88
Meter	89
Moving	90
Atomic Weight	91
The World	92
U-Crane	94
How To?	95
Steady Rainbow	96
Purple Irises	97
A Puzzle	98
Immigration	99
Notes	101

June 14, 2019
Ruxandra

As a Lily (I)

In response to Usha's book Rosary of Latitudes

If I told you, the rosary bewitched me,
it was a tender bridge in my brain
with several shamans crossing it
until the void was full of grace.
I found an inner power as a forgotten tissue
broidered once upon a time by our grandmothers.

The mastery of being as a crystal ship.

I destroyed loneliness with the glory of poetry,
starting a dervish dance in this poem,
twirling like never before
in the DNA of a pure future book.
Masters, lovers, seekers, givers, illuminated hominids,
All these people of hearts, vivid bones and scars,
how much I want to stay in a para-world,
in a new territory with no blame and shame.

I want to drink a wine like ink with you,
staying in a spiced sand.
I want to create a pilgrim agora for us,
a voyage song in an athanor.

Every poem could be a Jerusalem,
every verse, a diamond zone,
every word could be an intra-poem as a lily.

June 16, 2022
Ruxandra

As a Lily (II)

Seventeen words (my lucky number) about the world,

a carrousel with horses of live porcelain,
swinging butterflies in the head of a thousand poets.

I surpassed the words because of faith.

A lily is my mouth.

June 29, 2019
Ruxandra

Names (I)

Your name means *dawn*,
my name is *dawn*,
the same word is a gate,
like a sternum of a savaged heart for twins,
like the atriums for the oxygenated and deoxygenated.

There are not pulp fictions, dear dawn,
as my dawn is lightening your dawn
in a poem.
This is a story for tender lycanthropes,
with no teeth or claws.

Dawn is dawning in dawn.

June 29, 2019
Ruxandra

Names (II)

Little Sanskrit snakes and toys for sweet gods
are in this poem for two.
Let's play poetry like a ping-pong with pencils and books on fire.
This morning I dreamt of Ishtar,
she was not in Mesopotamia, but in India.

All the words were shining in my head,
but the brilliance was unsaid and untaken.
Then I knew I know nothing,
and this super-nothing was my wisdom.
Ishtar was an enlightened dark lady
in a little cage-poem at dawn.

July 1, 2019
Ruxandra

Names (III)

In my language your name means door.
It is a door to a meta-world
as I dreamt several years ago.
In my language which is not mine completely,
my name has the particle *man* inside.

Your door let me see myriads of names,
your door was an athanor.

In a language somewhat yours my name means shining,
it is the morning after the night
we both found the poetry of the other.

Your door let the morning come together
with all idioms and neurons,
your door was a window.

My name is a conqueror,
a soldier who loved an exotic queen.

This queen is probably poetry.

July 2019
Usha

Joysmos[1]

for Magda Cârneci & Ruxandra Cesereanu

"A reader will read us one day."
     —A Vast reader

These poems you write *write to* by which you tear scratch
carve delineate the universe on your terms
this   tug-of-war   with the world
your right   your triumph
your big   gulps of air   to live to breathe
to be   my sister-in-arms,

I am warmed in my bed now, I salute your poems
outside the dull-leaved oaks like ancient alligators
climbing to the sky, you bursting open the seams of words
as yellow pollen scatters in the air this very moment

outside my window,

I admit I do not know the trees or flowers in your country,
but here *morning glory, basket flower, coreopsis*
are shrill announcements calling my attention,
                              name us! they cry aloud,

in my bed now asking a thousand questions   the names
of your trees and flowers
what pollen is in your soul   your agonies
how regimes plunged into your bones

---

[1] Play on Magda Cârneci's book title *Chaosmos*.

and became the ink in your pen
and you sculpted your love stories   your souls

a cup of dark chocolate its aroma wafting
      on Victoria street   the street I walked
a few steps with you   and imagined
your revolts and victories,   the poem lost
in translation rising like an inviolate city on your pristine page,

your poems,   your poems breathing
in and out of the universe   order no different from chaos
no different from your violet emotions or red intellect
no different from your prayers no different from your politics no
different from your Godless deity no different from . . .

you write[2] *to*   me today,

you *write me. A reader will read us one day.*
Yes. Your waiting is over.

---

[2] *Write* is the major trope in both poets' work.

July 2019
Usha

Ushas

Goddess of dawn in Sanskrit

My consort is Surya, 'the sun',
chariot with seven horses,
spewing secret pāda of fire
in *anushtup,* awakening

hungry lotuses of action,
dazzling fairy tales begin
in heaven and plummet to earth,
my myth is I am harbinger

impeller, rouser of action,
in reality, my breath as
woman sours the breath of others,
my persistent light churns the world,

summons gods to hold its poison
in their throat, I end in twilight.
I am faint as a cobweb, I
warp volatile as a shadow,

my realm is the blink-light of stars,
the sibylline nests of branches,
moon singing ghazals of moonbeams,
rising with a thousand cool arms

to embrace the cosmos, my heart
a humming beehive with honey.

Pada: The basic metric unit/syllabic unit of Sanskrit poetry. Pāda (पाद)—refers to a "foot", or a "quarter" of a verse. Each *pāda* is made of a specific number of syllables.

Anushtup chanda: The *Aditya Hrudyaam,* a major Sanskrit hymn to the sun god is written in the anushtup meter. i.e., eight syllables in a *pāda* ('foot' or 'quarter-verse').

October 14, 2019
Ruxandra

Lotus

On losing her mother

My mother is a lotus,
every day I drop a Lancôme perfume from this lotus
every night this lotus is hashish and a treasure,
every morning is a mother inside my brain-heart.

October 14, 2019
Ruxandra

The Lost Lotus Found

Our dead are language,
our disappeared are poetry lodged in the heart,
our dissipated are invisible ink in the mind,
ourselves in themselves in yourselves.

My mother is a lotus,
every day I drop a Lancôme perfume from this lotus,
every night this lotus is hashish and a treasure,
every morning is a mother inside my brained heart.

She was my bird and my continent,
I was her breath and her struggle.
I regret not being her baby at 30
as Christ was still the baby of Madonna when he was 33.

Sometimes, in dreams, I beg her to stay in deep woods with me,
a stalker and a magus called Aurora,
eyes of a doe, creole hair, her shining face in the sky.
But she's not answering or if she does,
she's just an unseen bird of shadows.

My silver memories erased by not living as I was,
Paris, Rome, Madrid our pilgrim homes once upon a time,
My mother is a lost lotus which I want to tie in the waters.

She is my jar and my maze,
I am a girl looking for her fate after the rainbow died.
I am in transition, cutting out a second life.

What is a mother after her death,
What is a daughter after her life?

Matrix of snow in a lotus found, and home of findings.

November 2019
Usha

Both

I entered through a flaming looped gate,
one strand heaven, the other hell,
I have tried to unknot *me* from *her*,
one persists undeniably as the
Brahman's hum of bees,
from that urn of Love, I
came to be,
the other is bitten all over.

April 1, 2020
Usha

Ants

Home is a bird on a wire with the possibility of flight into dark woods or a patchwork of sky: it is the story of a daughter who had ants for pets as a child on one continent. On another, in Hyderabad, shallow breaths from resisting the inner matrix of mother; the serpentine struggle of the cellular to outdo itself, woman

becoming woman, and the woman in woeman's eternal dance inching toward gravity-free leaps. Home is the first battle zone always wet with the mother's blood; umbilical trail present even in new woods. Under her feet continents bloomed as lotuses. Hyderabad, that teeming city, gave her dreams surreal as blue ants.

By day, hypnotized out of the jar of earth, vicious ants trailed like dripping tar. Meandering meridians of a woman's destiny—her mother's sweats and nerves in Hyderabad's sun, furious as a chariot in war. Her escape from home to an inner labyrinth of somber shady woods, lost in underground mazes to distance her mother's

frenzied toiling above. Mostly, it was her mother's home. Her father silent as an anthill, his words, dark ants, surfaced as guerillas nested in dark woods. How could the daughter now as a married woman not recall the relentless heat and ants in that house as only pests? Snow now white as gamoxene—a hybrid heap of memories haunts—the cumulus of cities: Hyderabad Melbourne, Baltimore, White Plains, Austin. Madder than the hatter she feels transiting from house to house. What did the mother make of this child gentle with ants? She clung to the image like a grain of sugar. Now woman, the daughter fought to fly in spite of plummets in the woods.

Torn-winged, the futile fierce flutters that would not falter—a second best life! Shrapnel sticks—Hyderabad. The first war is the war that never ends. Can women ever cease perceiving their 'tragedy' as 'Mother?' They must be crushed—trailing memories brittle as ants, she hopelessly hopes to erase the thread that leads home.

April 1, 2020
Usha

The Lotus from Which I Ran Away

> "Within the city of Brahman, which is the body, there is the heart, and within the heart there is a little house. This house has the shape of a lotus, and within it dwells that which is to be sought after, inquired about, and realized. What then is that which, dwelling within this little house, this lotus of the heart, is to be sought after, inquired about, and realized?"
> —*Chandogya Upanishad* 8:1:1, 2

> "I am the knower . . . I was not born; I have neither body, nor senses, nor mind, I, the Supreme Self, dwell in the lotus of the heart. I am pure. I am One without a second."
> —Om Tat Sat, *Kaivalya Upanishad*

The deeper the mud, the more
beautiful the expected bloom of the lotus,
it is said from *samsara* rises the soul
supremely beautiful like a lotus—rather, *ought to rise,*
I suppose for us, one is the lotus,
the other the mire,
one rising out of the other,
moist mud oozing into a petalled-purity,

I suppose—it is you mother *who dwells within this little house.*

We are the two the metaphor holds,
the two things trying to become one, and failing.

So, I am in a box packed like tight sardines,
or cigars unlit—you are the box.

You are the house
from which I ran away

like a mouse,
not rising like the lotus of the supreme self.

I have felt myself to be without a second,
in a tunnel of loneliness,
and I've grown two tongues—of nectar and fire.

I grew like stalactites in your womb,
I am a fuse spluttering on both ends,
burning from

you.

April 8, 2020
Ruxandra

Rise Lotus, Rise Mother

Rise lotus from your waters in the shape of heart,
rise lotus from the house of deep heavens,
rise lotus from the sweet Brahman's brain,
rise lotus from the uncovered *Upanishad,*
rise lotus from the opened Self,
rise lotus and come to me.

I am the seeker, I am the dreamcatcher and the lantern.

Rise lotus, your petals are the footnotes of my life,
rise lotus, I am blooming from an unleashed love.

The metaphor of my love is in what I call lotus.

A mother is the mother of my love,
a love is the love of my house,
a house is the house of myself in the mother of love.

Love is a lotus in a mother.

No cigars or drugs, no gems or dangerous gifts,
just a lotus in a love poem.
An index for a tongue singing an extreme hymn forever.

Rise lotus, rise mother from the land of dead!
Your womb was a channel for my life to love,
the gates of burning waters in the shape of heart.

May 2020
Usha

Manthana

"Manthana" references the Hindu myth of the churning of the ocean

I want to write you a love poem mother,
How I want to write it,
On a page with angel wings,
a chalice of *amrit,*
holding a lullaby of us.

How then did we become
the churning waters?

May 13, 2020
Usha

This Is That

In response to a video reading by Ruxandra of a poem in Romanian

You read me a poem in Romanian
silhouetted in gray, stiff as a corpse
in a voice aged by the sky,
the light through the window is a shroud,

I listened.

A tree blooms in me with leaves of nameless colors,
of nameless terrors like the nameless dead
in Hart Island; the bodies of people dying
in battlefields of hospitals,
waging war with their bodies in lonely wards.

Is there a Hart Island in each of our souls
to dispatch the unclaimed debris of our lives?
Have we perfected the art of burial?

New lotuses rise from our underbelly,
all is a recycled menu from the eons.

Did I rise from my great grandfather, and he from a tree?
And the tree from his grandmother, and she from a snail?
And the snail from a fallen star
or broken home or murdered race?

Think about it, do not scoff at this poem,
Is your laughter shooting from grief's trunk?
And suffering a page from eternity's laughter?

May 14, 2020
Ruxandra

A Poem About a Poem

> *All the atoms in the air and in the desert are dancing,*
> *puzzled and bemused to the ray of light,*
> *they seem insane.*
>   —RUMI, "The poem of the atoms"

I stood at the window reading a poem about love,
not about the love of youth,
but of the holy maturity on its way to senectitude.

The world was outside and I
was inside like all transparent poets,
this is not a fashion and dogma,
this is grief, you are right,
you perfectly understood.

But in grief there is sometimes also tenderness,
I will never scoff at a poem
because a poem is the power within,
I will never kill or mock a lotus,
I inherited power and words from my beloved dead.

This is what I am doing now,
in this mixture of para-words and meta-words,
maybe even extra-words, sometimes.

Shroud, burial, corpse—these are not words for sale,
or to be enslaved in a panegyric,
these are delicate little poems
in a daydream about a healing shaman.

I try to heal myself,
this poem of atoms is a wanderer between us.

May 22, 2020
Usha

Yesterday, my friend,

I read Rumi, turning
page after page as I would
turn my ear to a child's laughter.

He has been some place
I have not,
that place outside of place,
time outside of time,
he knew a warmth
that does not come from fire
and *home* unbound from hearth.

Today, I doubt I am a poet,
my paltry mindscape a cloud in his sky,
I don't know the meaning of
the scatter of rabbits,
the conspiracies of the stars,
the contracts of the moon,
I doubt I am pilgrim,
I have missed
the lessons I must learn from the
handwriting of the sun,
and the lullaby of the night,
I've stood waiting on banks of echoes
For boats from wisdom's palace.

I too walked in the bazaar of Konya,
I did not hear the blacksmiths anvil,
I did not spiral in
the rhythm of a swirling heart,
or hear God's breathing in my wonder,

I woke up ordinary as the sheet on my bed.

Today, I want to give you
this poem as a calling card,
it may not reveal an address to *home,*
or be rail track for the train of your thought
but travel anyway, my friend

from a distant land,
where buildings rise like tortured dreams
from a fist of the past.

Today, I want
the world to be simple,
I want to be in an equation that need not be solved,

Simply, by my window
let me show you:

atoms of light between leaves,
leaves turned to mirrors,
mirrors turned to sun,
sun turned to a mouth of light
pouring into pupils
igniting

leaf to leaf
cell to cell
poet to poet
me
to
you
pointillistic
one.

May 24, 2020
Ruxandra

Lullaby

I must tell you how poetry stays in the entrails.

Once upon a time the window was my mouth,
once upon a time the doors were my mouth,
but then I found my proper mouth as the outcast organ of poetry.

Look at the window and you shall see a shadow of a lonely witch,
look at the doors and you shall see the ring of a pagan god,
feel the shadow and put the ring on your little left finger,
from here to there starts my lullaby,
my song of songs and of other songs,
this is a remake.

I do not doubt I am a poet,
but I know I'm not a shaman as I want so much to be.
Rumi was one of my first dervishes,
I discovered him in my remote coming-of-age,
he was dancing in my mind
and his legs were transparent verses,
I was dancing in his mind
and my legs were unseen verses,
a sweet brainwashing so as to save the inner world.

I am singing now,
I am dancing and may this lullaby,
be my heretic song and dance,
a poem inside a faraway poem,
a letter to myself so as to break on through
to the other side,
this is the other side, I am the other side,
A lullaby.

June 6, 2020
Usha

Between Us

(We open

days like the words of a lullaby
hours like pillows
night like a cradle
a deep sleep overtakes our poems

meanwhile

a country is dismembering itself
pressing its knee into its conscience

I will mail you this country as a letter
read it, tell me what it means
in your language
         here, I will grapple
with its foreign alphabet

with the hot embrace of summer heat
and flakes of cockroach wings, sweeping
their mute bodies & needle-thin antlers

spot fluffs of white and black flashing
as racoons skulk in the orange night
and an overtime light undulates gaudily
on the walls   do you hear our marches
in the snail of your ear?

Our children have been returned to our nests
no one understands the horoscope of the weather.

As I ponder the value of a comma against a period
uppercase vs lower—Allen Ginsberg is walking naked
in the capital with Kali by his side—
he unlocked the lockdown—followed
by plangent breath in the ventilators of masked-
marches—the air hemorrhages in cities—someone is
tuning the earth—resetting its chromosomes—people
pour into the streets—like oil from a canister—
streets like wicks, inflammable—
the brackets contain footnote-histories
—uncuffed   lynched
men are removing their nooses—
and a black rage burns hot white.

I am neither black or white
I am the color of uneasy peace
I am like a window pane between two realities
in this eternal osmosis for home
to the US: I return the credit card for borrowed time,
to India: my ashes, and ask the stars for another map.

and close
a bracket of us)

July 10, 2020
Ruxandra

Windows and Doors

Staying in one of my mother gowns, thinking it could be an immortal skin
and listening to Messiah of Händel so as to sweeten the sorrow.
Then reading your poem, your translucid letter, smelling your words.
Hallelujah! Hallelujah! Hallelujah! Hallelujah! Hallelujaaaaah!
The world is in iced flames and the personal ache is now just a zero.
I am white but I could be a black, red, yellow
or without a color, without a flag.
Not just a country, but the earth is slowly dismembering,
and the fringe are hanging near the rotten seams of melancholia.
Remember this prophet from half a century:
I saw the best minds of my generation destroyed by madness, starving hysterical naked,
these words are still pungent.
If India could be a Jerusalem and Jerusalem could be any other metropolis,
if cities, streets, mankind could change their ventricles.
This summer is not for time out, but for deep dream generator marches.

The carnival is not in Venice or Rio de Janeiro, but suspended or
    maybe perverted,
as the masks entered into the faces.
To think until the ashes, to be ready for a little Nirvana starting
    with ashes,
to be an astral ash one day.
Listen more to the prophet:
angel headed hipsters burning for the ancient heavenly connection
    to the starry dynamo in the machinery of night
We can be windows, we can be doors, always open.
We are the air, the breathing.
Poetry is the only way.
No maps, no servitudes, just transparence without any amoeba.

July 14, 2020
Usha

Piebald

1.

I read your poem
and burned all the flags fluttering in my heart,
I lowered 'India' then 'America' then 'South Asian'
then 'Woman' then 'Human being'—you get the picture
because you painted the scene with the brush of poetry
and took me to a land of nothingness!

Then,
I hoisted them again, one by one,
unafraid of their vain fluttering,
I *am* the wind the flag flutters in.

2.

Bushes bursting into flames,
stones growing tongues,
seas parting her thighs,
wheat murmuring in the breeze,
a man goes up the mountain
comes down a prophet,
and Jerusalem wails
her children looking away from each other.

In the land I was born,
they say Benares and Mecca,
the Nile and Ganges,
the cross and the swastika come and go
with the breath of the body;
on the banks of my consciousness
I cremate myself, on my cross I rise.

3.

In a dream, my grandmothers
rowed the boat on either end
on a black sea—it felt like
a loop of DNA—I was saddled between
a choiceless bestowing. Other things happened
in that dream, my father was washed away,
my mother absent—perhaps she was the boat;
the air, this life; my breath,
the poetry that got me through the journey.

July 17, 2020
Ruxandra

Questions

Devil is once again stuck
in the world with his reddish pigtail.
There are mixed questions for the beginners
and also for the veterans: why conspirators are seen like deities?
Even their illness is here-and-now a drowned dirty rainbow.
Why a strong genius is at the same time a fragile mortal
with sick words in his/her mouth?
We are dreaming of journeys by
boats, spaceships and other instruments for escape,
but mothers are dead in their sleep of nowhere and nobody.

Can we see things as they are in their transparent skin
not as they are in their spasm?
Even the spasm is today the formula and the supervisor.

My words are dry.

My words are judging the world in its visible entrails.

But where is the splendor of the Invisible?
Our eyes are wide-open-wide shut
like in a hide-and-seek game.

Checkmate, dear world and dear mortals,
you, hypocrite lecteurs, mes semblables, mes frères et sœurs.
We are in the tunnel and we shall remain here for a while.

October 8, 2020
Usha

Hello from America

walking in a tunnel,
tunnels, that are the veins of the goddess,
do you have a mother goddess?
is she in a crypt or in plain sight nursing God?

Calling from America,
Mother we are issuing you a visa,
Come.

October 10, 2020
Ruxandra

Hello, Goddess!

I remember I saw you in a famous metropolis.
You were an installation.

Thousands of inhabitants were waiting to glimpse you,
but not to touch you, because it was prohibited.

Goddess, you were not black as tar or *noire* as a movie.
Do not forget, poets are fertilizers.
So, what I am doing now is to fertilize your icon.

Dear Madonna of elephant dung and polyester
you were however pure gold.
My eyes are still blind because of that look once upon a time
and my body is caressed by the huge leaves of your cloak.

October 24, 2020
Usha

Map of the Mother

Pratipada, Day 1
Shailaputri/Bala Tripura Sundari

Celebrate red!
Welcome Shailaputri, Shakti-incarnate,
'Daughter of the mountain', consort of Shiva,
astride Nandi: mount of patience; armed for battle,
Parvati's, fearless spirit a burgeoning pink lotus.
Adorn *Bala Tripura sundari* armored by the great mother,
her life-surge slender as a vine drawn by swans,
her giggles fall as stars illumining the night sky,
Child, incarnadine my soul with your play!
*

The fireflies' hopscotch on an invisible grid,
the squirrel's erratic scamper-and-hide delights.

ॐ देवी शैलपुत्र्यै नमः ॥
Om Devi Shailaputryai Namah ॥

Dwitya, Day 2
Brahmacharini/Gayatri

Celebrate blue!
Parvati as Brahmacharini, the maiden
whose searing blue penance in hail and snow,
fading to a skeletal form ate leaves alone, and then none,
for this blue-tipped devotion, self-annihilation for Love,
Shiva had to concede and be claimed as her consort.

Adorn the three-eyed, five-headed *Gayatri* atop a red lotus,
teach me mastery, show me how to bloom
my carcass of hungers into a worship of flowers.
*
Outside, desire for the earth is falling from trees,
crackled brown leaves in hypnotic descent to her lap.

ॐ देवी ब्रह्मचारिण्यै नमः॥
Oṃ Devī Brahmacāriṇyai Namaḥ

Tritya, Day 3
Chandraghanta/Annapurna

Celebrate yellow!
Chandraghanta, temple-bell-forehead with the half-moon—
waning and waxing of eternity's serenade of chapters
time's fine-tipped arsenal seeping the universe,
she conquers its vagaries with immense resolve,
she assumes the terrifying to persuade him to gentler mien,
Annapurna Mother nourish me with food for the belly,
food for sustenance, food for endurance, food for comfort,
then, shape my *kamandalu* of appetites to hold your water.
*
I hear the rains have come there pounding furiously,
sweeping the streets like undulating pythons.

ॐ देवी चंद्रघण्टायै नमः ॥
Oṃ Devī Chandraghantaye Namaḥ

Chaturthi, Day 4
Kushmanda/Lalitha

Celebrate green!
Kushmanda, eight-armed light spilling in all directions!
The cosmic-egg spilled from the hint of her smile,
holder of jars of honey, birther of the golden sun,
beauteous *Lalitha,* golden womb of endless galaxies,
in her warmth: the earth flowers in emerald splendor,
opulent vegetation bursts, earth's fecundity burgeoning,
her juice overflows the veins of the cosmos,
universes bursting like ripe fruit on a bough.
*
The light drops its marigold garments on the ground,
shushes the shadows with its finery and ornaments.

ॐ देवी कूष्माण्डायै नमः॥
Oṃ Devī Kushmanda Namaḥ

Panchami, Day 5
Skandamata/Saraswati

Celebrate royal blue!
Skandamata, two-cheeked with peace and war,
Skanda, the war god, nestled as scar of her own skin,
four-armed great mother, wielding wielders of weaponry,
blooming with the musk of lotuses, of life's
lust for life, waging endless battles for peace,
worship *Saraswati, vag devi,* goddess of speech,
originator of sound blooming as effulgent petals,
vein me mother with melodies the bees know.

*

The cerulean sky thrums with melodies silent in my veins,
this blue-hued stranger eavesdrops on my heart's desires.

ॐ देवी स्कन्दमातायै नमः ॥
Oṁ Devī Skandamātāyai Namaḥ

Sashti, Day 6
Katyayini/Mahalakshmi

Celebrate vermillion red!
Katyayini, refulgent daughter of the flames,
blood-thirsty slayer of savage buffalo patriarchy,
woman in full form mounted on a lion-heart,
swollen anger, matured life-force, full-blooded,
lightening streaked valiance to restore the sacred feminine,
nectar-heart of compassion and forgiveness.
Mahalakshmi, reveal how my heart is a treasure chest,
the philosopher's stone within, the searched for grail.
*
Unstoppable tumbling tangerine antics of the sun,
irreverent to fluttering flags of autumn's wind.

ॐ देवी कात्यायन्यै नमः ॥
Oṃ Devī Kātyāyanyai Namaḥ

Saptami, Day 7
Kalaratri/Durga Devi

Celebrate white and black!
Kalaratri Durga great destroyer, you say, 'I rise
on the ash-smeared corpse of day,
your breath coils up as incense to join my void,
your poems dance on the cremation ground of your life,
every baby encased in every woman's flesh
is a reminder of the universe in my womb,
History itself spat out of me, nothing is blasphemous,
my black is the white of your salvation.'
*
Outside, long tar road like the tongue of Kali,
the taste of lives waking up on her palette.

ॐ देवी कालरात्र्यै नमः ॥
Oṃ Devī Kālarātryai Namaḥ

Ashtami, Day 8
Mahagauri/Mahishasuramardini

Celebrate pink!
Mahagauri, the sacred-feminine destruction
subsides, she sloughs her dark rage,
emerges shining, shimmering, golden
on a white bull with tambourine, we too
darken and lighten our hearts palpitations in cycles,
unafraid embrace our dual essence, you too!
women come on roaring mounts, you too!
Flood the streets, you too! Me too! Me too! Strike!
*
The sky like a tamed bull, placid and cloudless,
the goddess astride in pink lotus-clouded sari.

ॐ देवी महागौर्यै नमः॥
Oṃ Devī Mahagauri Namaḥ

Navami, Day 9
Siddhidhatri/Raja Rajeswari

Celebrate purple!
Siddhidhatri, grant us ultimate insight
holding up your mirror, show us who we are,
composite sexed, male and female,
Ardhanarishwar, delight in the reflection
neither wanting to exert dominance or be dominant,
Raja Rajeswari salutations! Reasonless mercy!
In the temple of this multi verse her secret doctrine,
primordial mystery petal-aligning in triangular emanations!
*
Fiery vermillion dot resplendent on the sky's darkling brow,
She rises and sinks in glory in petalled sky of jasper-hued clouds.

ॐ देवी सिद्धिदात्री नमः॥
Oṃ Devī Siddhidatri Namaḥ

Visarjan, Day 10
Durga Visarjan

Celebrate! I pause
my circuitry of time and eternity,
an unbloomed lotus,

an arrow suspended on a bow,
a jar of unspilled elixir,
an unthrown trident,
a still wheel,
my arms of desire at rest,
Dissolve! Peace! Peace! Peace!
*
Inscrutable night reclines in deep slumber,
anklets of light and unknown stirrings in her womb.

October 2020
Ruxandra

9 Days of Poetry

1.

I dreamt about Bengal.
I was feverish talking to a buffalo
whose mouth was on fire.
Usha-in-sari came in my dream and said:
let's go to the festival,
let's make a graceful liaison.
Then a water goddess arose and put the bones of the world
    together.

2.

Every goddess is my mother deep down.
Every goddess is herself but also the curly uterus I came from.
Every buffalo is a challenge for making poetry a good fight.

3.

There is no mud in poetry.
Even in mud it could be light.
Chiaroscuro. A technique of the heart's eye.

4.

I am saying for the first time this name: *Lalitha*.
This new name for me is the birth of a new poem.
I am an insider.

5.

This is a hymn to bond the human heart inside.
This is a hymn to worship amity.
This a hymn into a hymn.
A Matryoshka nesting doll.

6.

A mantra genealogy:
in the beginning there was a child,
then a teenager,
then a young heart,
then a grown-up,
then a grey-haired stranger
and once again a newborn.
Many birds.

7.

Sometimes I know the lotus is a room.
No door, no windows, just a room.
A monk's cell or even better a nun's cell.

8.

I utter the phonemes of several goddesses.
AUM.
It is my bird song.
My tremor of tunes.

9.

Nine days of poetry, in the mood for searching for a Sanskrit goddess, and the Madonna of our Lord. And my dead mother Aurora. Her crystal name, and the lotus of the nine days were the lens to have her back to life in my words.

March 3, 2021
Usha

Dredge

The goddess says
dredge the secret of the stars
smelling of jasmine
with alphabet of hibiscus-red.

So, if the needles & the yarn,
& the knitter is a stalk of silence,
the rest is chatter,

—her light on my face,
if I turn to the music of trees,
the bread of friendship,
the Monalisa smile of a baby,
the lip of the red rose,
the impatience of the river,

will the dots of my life add up to a rangoli?
will I be a line in the house of triangles?

The Madonna is silent in my yard,
it is days since I lit a lamp for her,
the flame-tipped hours instead
wobble unevenly in her name,
I join her name to the thousand names of *Lalitha,*
I know she won't mind;

she's trailed her cape in eternity,
the sun bows to her patience,
I destroy idols in her name,
seek her teething
            in the grass's whispers.

March 6, 2021
Ruxandra

A Lost/Forgotten Poem

Your poem reminded me of a lost poem of mine
(or maybe a forgotten poem in a day-dream)
about the Virgin of the Sparrows.
She is an inner Madonna that I invented for my needs.
Once upon a time I talked to Her in versets,
but now I remember only some letters:
Your breast is pure silver
and I saw sparrows on a morning-spring
coming from You.
Your sparrows entered my mouth,
their taste was ambrosia,
then lights arose inside my body
and my hair was burning like a nightly torch.
I had a star in me, called Absinth,
this name came from nowhere in the Bible.
The sparrows in my mouth were nuns,
their monastic skin was silk.
My eyes were feverish like a walnut forest.
Then I heard the bell flower
of a small wooden church dancing on the hill.

May 11, 2021
Usha

Then Lights Arose in Memory

In the amber light a penumbra of shadows
rises and falls on walls,
the sting of mosquitoes jolts us,
the siren of the pressure cooker singes skin,
in a routine power-cut,
the heat quilts the room.

The petal of flame holds steady
in the cup of the lantern's glass,
from his shy mouth emerge winged things—
Hindi songs testing flight in the darkness,
the songs flicker their wings,
waning waxing on an underwater
of too many denials in life,
the air curves as a conch shell around him,
the curtains are shadowy waterfalls,
ancestors breathing in our midst.

His living has been diminutive,
apologetic for the space he takes on earth,
in this light he is poised to be something
other than ordinary,
in the milky way he momentarily shines

on the filigree of memory, then lights arise—
father whose tread has been soft on the earth
whose breath I ex/inhale.

August 9, 2021
Ruxandra

Lantern

Changing words in poetry is like changing position in utero.
In heaven and underground.
I'm nesting a lantern now in my brain,
equalizing uterus with cerebrum or with heart.
What a thesaurus through language!
A trunk with objects and passions.
But now I am taking the lantern
and shining it on all the extremities of the world.
Searching for my trunk, for my orbit,
changing words like changing position in utero
I see the sparkling lights.

September 2021
Usha

Aialik

I offered myself
to the exactitude of the meeting;
the wind scalding my face,
arresting debris of thought,
condensing time.

A jagged conglomerate of
ice blue and white—it loomed—
a great tongue loose between mountains,
she he it silenced all language,
Joy! Awe! Joy!
Gigantic uterine outpour,
unleashed—a liquid abyss,
the glacier shedding its skin with a primal roar—
remnants blobbing in the water—
sculptures in white misshapen perfection—

And life here too!
Otter, seal, sea lion—winged smear hovering on crag—

the force that shaped this,
shaped this meeting too—
this enormity of nature
fitting into my eye-scape,
Rumi's echo—*the soul of man*
that fits all things in its own movements
or the things it beholds?

October 5, 2021
Ruxandra

Bodies of Poems

We had a zoom-dialogue about how a goddess
or a mother can be a body of a poem.
It is precisely a navel.
What a drunk word is *life-death,*
what an unknown song of songs.
I do not have another indestructible concept.
Maybe this poem is a little magic box.
Let's share other bodies of poems.
Let's share.

October 6, 2021
Usha

Meet Me in the Mirror

Let's share
a trail of lights
& distant chants,

on a blue arctic screen,
tongues flaring with words
& primal mess,

She is the body
of the poem,
ethics & anti-ethics,

Meet me in the mirror
of this poem,
reflect!

Hear her musical
anklets in the poem,
Dance!

October 7, 2021
Ruxandra

Whirlpools

I shall dance.
I shall chant.
I shall be the body of a poem.
You are also a body of a poem.
Between us are mothers and goddesses living.
I shall meet you in the mirror,
changing new versets and psalms.
Aurora Borealis is the background of our poems,
a metaphor, of course, for the groundwater of the mind.
Now we are in the Land of Tropes.
Floating, swimming, hovering.
Blooming in a myriad of greenish, bluish and cyclamen
    whirlpools.

October 12, 2021
Usha

Meru

It is the season of the goddess again,
each morning, I rise, shower off the drivel
of hours, and drive to the temple;
the priest chants the Devi's names placing
marigolds and roses on the *Meru,*
nine times my hope ascends
a pearly pink mountain.
I dress my faith in a sari with hues
of the cosmos, studded with glittering stars
bordered by shiny rivers.
nine times my lotus
of faith, petalled with her names.

October 19, 2021
Ruxandra

The Show Must Go On

Maybe it is a menhir what we are building here.
After all, menhirs are not built only by stone,
but by words and hymns.
In another life it could be
The Konark Sun Temple
or Notre-Dame de Paris
 or The Temple of Solomon,
a girlish way of day-dreaming,
mixing space and time in poetry.

The first ray of light is falling at the entrance.
Then we see the menhir:
it is a lace.
I am a lacework and I summon you to follow me.
The show must go on.

November 13, 2021
Usha

Menhir

Menhir. A word is like a chime or pickaxe,
it excavates layers of memory,
a finger, it turns pages of a childhood,
stops here:
Asterix and Obelix—
clumsy Obelix with red pigtails
was always carrying menhirs
to do some Druid Gaulery,
frowning Asterix, cerebral
and sure like a branch,
relied on common sense—these
two ended up compatible as
opposites usually are.

There are also other pages
from the remote snowy
mountains of childhood:
Tintin and Snowy
Calvin and Hobbes;
a young man with a talking dog,
a stuffed tiger talking to a child;

and now, we talking
to the images of our childhood,
hoping for them to come alive.

November 20, 2021
Ruxandra

A Killer Instinct

We did not know that someday childhood will become old age,
our language was not trained for that.
When we were kids, King Kong was a cinematic
beast for the fragile stage of midgets,
like a book with an index for nightmares.
But long before King Kong, it was the playful heart of Mowgli
and the hominid animals that helped him to become a master of the
    world.
We were bitter-sweet champions together with Mowgli,
we were imaginary friends with the animals around him.
I feel like Mowgli now on his way from maturity to caducity,
and like in stained glass I have a glimpse of my first years.
We were Alice in her realms.
We were Peter Pan in his heavens.
For a long time, poetry was my companion,
I believed in poetry more than in anything else.
The poet must be a beast and have a killer instinct for words—
this is my ultimate sentence related to brain, heart and language.
I wrote these lines thirty years ago and I still believe in them.

January 15, 2022
Usha

Happy New Year

Happy new year says
Omicron, new avatar
in a global co
             mic

book, that brings no laughs.

January 16, 2022
Ruxandra

What Else Can Be Said

this is a poem written in a language other than the one I speak and I have never spoken before, although I once knew it, forgot it, relearned it and here I am writing again.

I'm writing again in this language; I'm taking it from the beginning and I'm learning the first letters.

until I reach the last letters it is a way of a life or two.

a poem can only be written in a forgotten language; then one day it wakes up from the dust, finding its new colors.

a new language is always an old language.

I am still human?

January 24, 2022
Usha

Until I Reach the Last Letters
It Is a Way of a Life or Two

I will begin with the word-of-the-day:
exiguous: very small in size or amount;
a little pain in life can erase a lifetime of pleasure
a little word, a relationship,
a little prescription, a disease,
a little virus, humanity—or its re-discovery,

a little screen, faces of hope

a little poem—*us.*

January 25, 2022
Ruxandra

Adults in Conversation

This is a special lullaby for adults.
No more tropes,
just a phrase for the beginning of something:
friendship and love, the only acid trip now,
even a rave party inside the isolation.
Look how the figures of speech resuscitated their pavements.
Where are the hard particles for our language?
Pandemic words for a post-pandemic poetry.

January 24, 2022
Usha

Until I Reach the Last Letters
It Is a Way of a Life or Two

I will begin with the word-of-the-day:
exiguous: very small in size or amount;
a little pain in life can erase a lifetime of pleasure
a little word, a relationship,
a little prescription, a disease,
a little virus, humanity—or its re-discovery,

a little screen, faces of hope

a little poem—*us.*

January 25, 2022
Ruxandra

Adults in Conversation

This is a special lullaby for adults.
No more tropes,
just a phrase for the beginning of something:
friendship and love, the only acid trip now,
even a rave party inside the isolation.
Look how the figures of speech resuscitated their pavements.
Where are the hard particles for our language?
Pandemic words for a post-pandemic poetry.

January 25, 2022
Usha

Meter

We may call this a diphthong of a poem
originating in me ending in you
or vice versa . . .

What is the meter of friendship
or a pandemic? Or fatigue?
What shall we stress and unstress
as the world finds words to write itself
as it mutates endlessly?

February 9, 2022
Ruxandra

Moving

We are moving in words like in rubber beds
or rather like in insectarium.
Sometimes a poem can save a life,
but it can't save the world.

If you put the letters in a Mendeleev Table and mix them up,
the earth will be an acoustic chemistry.
And then you wonder where the poetry is,
where it travels, through what throats,
through how many cerebrums.

But there is still friendship and love and sharing—
The Holy states of the poets, what a honeyed utopia!
I'm a believer and I don't want to lose this gift.

June 14, 2022
Usha

Atomic Weight

What is the atomic weight of war
in the periodic table of countries?

June 15–16, 2022
Ruxandra

The World

The world we live in,
the world around us,
no dementia was ticked off in the mirror until it was too late,
sometimes the image of a downcast child is more crushing
than an exploding tank or a burning building,
we don't need an open wound or a torn body to understand,
just see old people hidden in an underground,
in a shelter, crammed into each other,
not knowing why their lives have changed,
the limit of harsh images is what is happening
and yet, images are necessary to be unfolded and seen.
Ignorance and indifference are harmful
and impotence is grinding,
savage images are overwhelming,
we look, we are shocked, disturbed,
we look, pause, and we look.

Difficult to write and talk about,
so much loss it's hard to process,
something terrible is happening,
and then something terrible is happening again.

Survivors begging for the corpses of their loved ones,
the pain is dull because it is so great,
what is frightening is that death no longer causes pain,
the impossibility to mourn
if the corpses are not returned,
living people afraid that the dead will be killed a second time.

June 6, 2022
Usha

U-Crane

"Territory defense is either acoustic with both birds performing the unison call, or more rarely, physical with attacks usually by the male . . . Rarely, breeding territorial crane pairs allow a third crane into the territory to form polygynous or polyandrous trios that improves the chances of survival of the pair's chicks."

—Wikipedia entry on cranes

The crane can make no U-turn now
it flies débris to débris
it reached out long,
opportunistic, brave,
lacerated

Its map—an image of a chick before flight,
on its borders polygynous alliances.

Threatened and
now critically endangered.

Sedentary, it shows its migratory form
a land seeped of people
bleeding into borders, roosting in new lands.

Most species of cranes have been affected by human activities and are at the least classified as threatened, if not critically endangered. Metaphor for Ukraine in the poem.

How To?

July 3–Sep 1, 2022
Ruxandra & Usha

The words as knives out in an ataraxic brain,
I don't know how to heal the vast Ukrainian pain. (R)

Luhansk has fallen! one more firepower from the history of war,
Too many tracks on the geography of human conquest and defeat.
    (U)

Once upon a time it was *termendum fascinosum,*
Nowadays it is *tremendum horrendum.* Just *tremendum* is the
    same. (R)

The world is a Rubik cube forever seeking monochrome,
Few solve the riddle, some on unicycles with barely make it. (U)

A little girl with autism smiling in her mother phone-camera,
Then nothing, but torn flesh, this is the Ukrainian hurt in chain. (R)

My offerings dwindle as our words osmosis in the goblet of this
    poem,
My thirst slackens, friend. (U)

August 2, 2022
Ruxandra

Steady Rainbow

For Andrei Zanca

There is a grace in love,
but sometimes there is also a grace in death.
And this last grace is
like a steady rainbow raised above the world of the living,
as if the sky watched the perishing embraces for many years.
The flame still burns,
but this fire no longer smolders,
and the words are like bridal veils.
There is a grace in death that we ought to learn in life.
And there is a cloistered solitude of grace
that only the dying can glimpse and witness.
We, the living, can only wait.

August 2, 2022
Usha

Purple Irises

For Andrei Zanca

Your poem fell like snow on the audience that evening,
words stitched a gossamer gold mantle,
there was a yearning for peace and heaven in your offering,
close-up, the air around you folded in an origami of
fearsome
purple
bruised irises,
plucked, they remain folded tight in the crevice of memory.

You were lost and losing with angel wings,
you wore an invisible cape of death and prophecies,
your eyebrows like bats in flights,
your utterances—gibberish, spells, poetry, wishes, witchery—and
    prayer,
I knew you too little to stake a friendship,
or to mourn now,
I hope where you are,
there is gentle rain and blossoms you deserve,
I hope the snow has melted.

September 28, 2022
Ruxandra

A Puzzle

Poetry, war, death, pain, disease, love, closeness, a puzzle,
opposite things hanging on the tree of life,
again and again, exhaustion on a spiral.
The seasons and stars curled up in crystal nest.
The words grow like a bodyguard
building no asylum, only poetry.
It's a slide show where parts of the world have gone crazy.
We finally skinned the crust of despair,
we still believe in the power of idioms.

March 31, 2022
Usha

Immigration

For Ruxandra, for "Ants and Lotus"

I've wondered how to close our communion,
when I read: six people of Romanian and Indian
descent were found dead in a marsh near the Canada-US border.

There are others aligning like us.

We too have been rowing a boat trying to
illegally sneak into a new country,
on a boat with ghosts of rowers.

We've made many crossings, I hope.

We were reaching for a territory with no name,
there was rain, sleet, and strong wind—they
went by other names: covid, death, loss.

Will we capsize?
Will there be an autopsy,
toxicology tests?

Become undocumented asylum seekers?

Will we expand the pathway for legal entries?

Notes

Ruxandra, "Names I"

Usha researched the name 'Ruxandra' derived from the Old Persian "Roušanak / Roshanak" meaning bright, dawn, window of light, or shining.
'Usha' derives from 'Ushas,' the goddess of dawn in Sanskrit.
The bridge was in place.

Usha, "Hello from America"

Dear Ruxandra,

I must believe there is a rhythm and timing for everything. I must say a little about the new short poem that came naturally. I just finished reading a brilliant book by Neela Saxena—*Absent mother God of the West*. Neela traveled all across Europe looking for the Black Madonna relating her to Kali the Indian goddess. She like many feminist scholars basically hopes that understanding, accepting and incorporating the sacred feminine will help heal our souls and planet. I have condensed the book to two lines but it is so much more. There is a line of thought that the absence of a female god in Christianity gave rise to patriarchy in the West . . .

So, the poem came naturally from the emotions of the book. I start my poem where your poem ended: with tunnels; tunnels are black, the color of Kali and the black Madonna which is the color of the 'pregnant void' from which comes all creation containing both genders.

Ruxandra, "Hello, Goddess"

Dear Usha,

Thank you very much for the story you told me here so as to understand your poem. I have also a story for my little poem as a response. In 2000, I saw in New York an extraordinary exhibition called Sensation, with young artist from UK. The majority of the art products were installations. It was also a Madonna made by polyester, raisin and elephant dung. It was iconic. But one of the visitators of the exhibition throw a spray on it so to destroy it because . . . it was blasphemy. It was not a blasphemy at all. My poem is inspired by this image.

Usha, "Map of the Mother"

The Navratri festival represents a symbolic/archetypal battle that takes place between the warrior goddess Durga and Mahishasura, the buffalo demon and other male demons. The nine days celebrate the nine splendid forms of the goddess and her victory over evil. Each day of the nine days depicts one form of the goddess. On the tenth day the towering idols in the state of Bengal are submerged in water. In her ultimate form as Lalitha, she is considered the grand creatrix of the universe (s) birthing gods and goddesses, of form and formless divinity— she represents the shakti or force/energy/strength of the gods— and all of manifested creation. Numerous different Sanskrit hymns exist praising her various forms, extolling her manifold aspects. A color a day is allotted to her and it seems it is arbitrary though each color is symbolic of virtues and aspects.

In 2020, Navratri commenced on October 17th to October 26th. Coincidentally, I had read Neela Saxena's *Absent mother God of the West,* just prior to Navratri and the goddess symbolism was on my mind; I alluded to it in my poem 'Hello' to which Ruxandra responded with 'Hello, Goddess' in which she mentions ta Madonna exhibit in NYC. Bang in the midst of Navratri, the goddess had to be called for fully, it seemed to me. And so, this poem was written, a direct paean to her without a more modern interpretation.

The writing of the poem became my form of worship to celebrate the sacred feminine divine principle. The poem maps the goddess's manifestation from child—bride—mature woman—dissolution in the last stanza—spanning all perceived dualities. Each stanza is nine lines with an additional tenth couplet to mirror the span of the festival. I invoke the representative goddess in the poem as defined by tradition as well as the goddess adorned and decorated in the Austin Hindu temple, on each day of Navratri thus referencing my present— followed by an observation of nature or prakriti in the present moment in Austin. I conclude with a final invocation of the Sanskrit mantra for each goddess.

August 2, 2022: Ruxandra Cesereanu: When I met Usha, in 2019, in Bucharest, it was a destined poetic encounter. Our book was born from this special encounter and represented an intense dialogue. But in Bucharest we both met another poet, perhaps in an equally fateful sense. Andrei Zanca. Fascinated by Usha's presence, by her tender exoticism, as a poet and woman, Andrei was our poetic companion for a few hours.

I knew Andrei from his and my youth, but we rarely met, every ten years maybe. In 2019, we dialogued in threes, curious about each other, not only poetically, but also humanly. And Andrei predicted, at one point, a fatal illness to Usha. Usha and I were amazed by this prediction, it was something strange, completely unusual, shocking us. I, at least, projected that prophecy as poetic gibberish. But something happened. In 2022, Andrei died of a fatal illness, so the prophecy that surprised Usha and me, in some symbolic or metaphorical way may actually have been about himself. After Andrei's death, I read one of his last poems which was on death, on separation from those close, but also on gratitude. Especially the theme of gratitude troubled me in this poem which I also sent to Usha to read. So, the poems *Steady Rainbow* (written by me) and *Purple Irises* (written by Usha) are a posthumous dialogue with Andrei Zanca.

About Usha Akella

Usha Akella, was a finalist for Austin's poet laureate in 2025. She has authored twelve books (poetry and plays) published by notable publishers such as the Sahitya Akademi, India and Spinifex Press, Australia. She holds three Masters, the most recent an MSt in Creative Writing from the University of Cambridge, UK in 2018. Her poems have been translated into Romanian (upcoming), Macedonian and Spanish; notable, is the Mantis Editores (Mexico) Spanish translation of *The Waiting* by Elsa Cross. She was a Creative Ambassador for the City of Austin for 2019 & 2015.

She is the founder of *Matwaala* (www.matwaala.com) dedicated to amplifying the visibility of South Asian diaspora poets in the U.S.A. Her work under this umbrella has gained wide recognition. She is co-host of www.the-pov.com, a website of curated interviews. She has been published in approximately 150 journals and anthologies, and featured at numerous international poetry festivals in Romania, Macedonia, Slovenia, Slovakia, Mexico, India, Colombia, Nicaragua etc.

She is the editor of *Hum Aisecih Bolte! This is just how we speak* an anthology on the city of Hyderabad (2023), a festschrift on Keki N. Daruwalla published by the Sahitya Akademi (India's academy of letters) in 2024, and the co-editor of the 2025 version of the historic *Shri Sai Satcharita,* a hagiographic biography of the revered saint Shirdi Sai Baba.

About Ruxandra Cesereanu

Ruxandra Cesereanu is one of the most important contemporary Romanian writers. She was born in Cluj on August 17, 1963. Over the last two decades, she has been writing poems and novels lauded with a number of literary honors. She is also a professor in the Department of Comparative Literature at Babeș-Bolyai University and staff member of the Center for Imagination Studies at the Phantasma institute, serving as director of the creative writing workshops on poetry, prose and screenwriting.

Cesereanu's work displays strong influences from the Surrealist, Expressionist and Postmodernist traditions. Her experimental poetry uses psychoanalytic techniques to create collages, in which femininity and eroticism, life and death play large roles.

Her work is not only very personal but civic. Cesereanu has experienced the uprising and fall of the Romanian communist regime. She has written about Romanian politics and is known for her civic activist work.

Cesereanu's poetry has been translated mostly in English (5 books published in USA) and Italian (2 books published by Aracne Publishers, in Rome) but also in Hungarian, German and French. She recently published *California (on Somes),* translated by Adam J. Sorkin (Black Widow Press, Boston, 2023). Her achievements have been noted in *Who's Who in Contemporary Woman's Writing*, edited by Jane Elridge Miller (Routledge, London and New York, 2001) and Harold B. Segel, *The Columbia Literary History of Eastern Europe since 1945* (Columbia University Press, New York, 2008).

www.ingramcontent.com/pod-product-compliance
Lightning Source LLC
Chambersburg PA
CBHW072049160426
43197CB00014B/2692